GEORGIAN STYLE AND DESIGN
FOR CONTEMPORARY LIVING

GEORGIAN STYLE AND DESIGN
FOR CONTEMPORARY LIVING

HENRIETTA SPENCER-CHURCHILL

CICO BOOKS

LONDON NEW YORK

First edition published in 2008 by CICO Books

This edition published in 2012 by CICO Books
An imprint of Ryland Peters & Small
20–21 Jockey's Fields
London WC1R 4BW

5th Floor, 519 Broadway,
New York, NY 10012

www.cicobooks.com

10 9 8 7 6 5 4 3 2 1

ISBN: 978 1 908862 29 7

Printed in China

Project editor: Alexandra Parsons
Editor: Alison Wormleighton
Designer: Christine Wood
Photographer: Christopher Drake

contents

The Georgian period, in my view, was the most influential and enlightening of architectural eras and is one that has stood the test of time. Governed by classical principles of design, particularly those involving scale and proportion, it is a style of both exterior and interior that is immensely pleasing to the eye. The attention to the detail of each and every architectural element is what I find particularly intoxicating. Whether you are restoring an existing eighteenth-century property or looking to build or furnish a new house in Georgian style, there is a wealth of reference and a plethora of wonderful designs and gifted craftsmen to help you achieve your aims.

In this book you will see examples of the renovation of Georgian houses showing how period rooms have been modernized to make them practical for twenty-first century living. We illustrate the restoration of period features and show how, if replacements are needed and if they are carried out in a sympathetic manner, you can retain a period home's existing character.

In addition, you will find examples of several major new-build homes, all in the Georgian style. These not only show the influence and glory of the eighteenth century but also demonstrate how classical features and architectural details can be successfully reproduced to emulate the past. Colour, pattern, texture and accessories will all help to bring harmony and life to a room, but these are insignificant if the 'bones' are not in place. By this I mean the room's structure – its proportions and architectural details such as windows, doors, architraves, plasterwork and wall and floor finishes – and how all these elements relate to one another. This understanding of structure was the glory of Georgian style.

By studying great buildings from the Georgian era and absorbing influences from the many great craftsmen of the time, I have greatly enjoyed putting what I have seen into practice through working on both old and new houses – and I hope this book will help you in your quest to do the same.

Henrietta Spencer-Churchill

the classic
georgian house

When we think of the Georgian house, we see in our mind's eye a country mansion of elegantly symmetrical proportions placed perfectly in a landscape, or a magnificent terrace of town houses adorned with railings and porticos and classical columns. In fact, the Georgian period, which spanned the reigns of England's first four King Georges and lasted for more than a century (1714–1830), evolved over the years. Along the way it encompassed a variety of styles, from the rigidly classical idiom of the Roman temple to the exuberant swags and other ornament of the rococo period. What all manifestations of Georgian style had in common, however, was an obsession with quality of craftsmanship and with the creation of a balanced stylistic whole. A fitting manifesto, I think, for any architect or interior designer.

ABOVE: Image of Houghton Hall, Norfolk, from Colen Campbell's book *Vitruvius Britannicus*. Campbell drew up the original design for the house in 1721.

LEFT: Nostell Priory, West Yorkshire, is an 18th-century architectural masterpiece. It was built in 1735–50 by James Paine, and was completed by Robert Adam in 1766–76. The interiors are among Adam's best work.

the classical ideal

The evolution of Georgian houses in eighteenth-century Britain was both rapid and diverse thanks to a building boom fuelled by an emerging and wealthy middle class. Many of the early Georgian houses were built not by trained architects, but by well-educated 'men of taste'. Recently returned from their European travels on the 'Grand Tour', these gentlemen amateurs were inspired by the tenets of classical Roman architecture, as described and prescribed by the sixteenth-century Italian architect Andrea Palladio. Spurred on by a new political will to forge a British identity, Palladianism became the British national style.

The admiration for classical ideals and an architecture of 'antique simplicity' was expressed in houses with beautiful proportions and symmetry. Palladian principles underpinned the architecture not just of the grandest homes but also of more modest villas and terraced houses. Emphasis was placed on the exterior, initially with scant regard for the practicality of the interior layout. Many of the style changes that occurred were owing to a desire for more comfort, but the fundamental principles altered little through the Georgian period.

The Georgian era can be loosely divided into three periods: early Georgian (1714–1760), mid-Georgian (1760–1800), and late Georgian (1800–1830). The late

BELOW: Chiswick House, in west London, is one of the most glorious examples of Palladianism. It was never intended as a residence but was designed by the leader of the Palladian revival, Lord Burlington – the 'architect Earl' – as a temple of the arts, where he could display his collections of books and works of art and could entertain friends. Inspired by Palladio's Villa Rotunda in Vicenza, Italy, it was built in 1726–29. William Kent was responsible for much of the interior decoration of this Palladian gem.

Georgian period takes in the Regency period, named after the Prince Regent, who ruled England for nine years prior to becoming King George IV in 1820. In reality, all these periods overlapped and influences were seen in different parts of the country at different times.

Georgian houses were built of stone or brick, depending on local availability. In the cities of Bath and Edinburgh, for example, stone was plentiful and so it was commonly used for building, whereas in London the houses were mostly brick.

the palladian house

A typical early Georgian Palladian house consisted of an oblong symmetrical facade with a door in the centre surmounted by a pediment supported by columns or pilasters. To each side was a series of white-painted double-hung sash windows, which were repeated on the floors above. A Venetian window – an arched window flanked by two narrow rectangular windows – was often a focal point above the door. The hipped roof was partially hidden behind a parapet.

The tallest windows, and the main rooms, were on the *piano nobile* (the principal floor, above the ground floor), often accessed by a grand external staircase.

BELOW: Town houses in Queen Anne's Gate, one of London's best-preserved streets of 18th-century houses. Uniform window and door treatments gave the simple architecture an elegance that is still much appreciated today.

ABOVE: The Royal Crescent, Bath, is one of the best examples of urban Georgian architecture in Britain. Designed by the architect John Wood the Younger and built in 1767–75, it was the first crescent in Britain and was copied in many towns around the country. The giant Ionic columns rise from a plinth formed by the plain ground floor. The Bath stone blocks were laid so the joints are almost invisible.

These rooms, which conformed to strict mathematical proportions based on the cube, led off a large central hall. This was often double-height and lit from above by a skylight or dome. The ground floor housed the service rooms, informal living rooms and possibly the kitchen, while the attic rooms were reserved for children and servants. Some houses had symmetrical wings attached by a colonnade or single-storey corridor, for the kitchen and stables.

the georgian terrace

In towns and cities similar classical principles were applied to terraces, crescents, squares and circuses. A grand block of terraced houses (row houses), such as those in the city of Bath, might be designed as a continuous frontage, with a central pedimented section flanked by terraced houses and assemblages of columns, creating a 'palace' facade. Again, the main rooms were on the *piano nobile*.

More modest town houses were also built, and they, too, were fundamentally Palladian. As time went on, continuity along the entire terrace became more widespread, with uniform elements such as pediments, canopies or porticos, windows and pilasters. The scarcity of building land meant that the houses were relatively narrow and two to four storeys high.

During the mid-Georgian period, newly built town houses did not differ radically from their early Georgian predecessors, though the detailing was more delicate and uniform. The palace facade with its central pedimented section was used increasingly. Sash windows became more elongated, so that the windows of town houses were of almost equal height on each floor. Though the glazing bars were more delicate, the windows were often highlighted with contrasting stone or brick surrounds and were given deeper reveals. Upstairs windows had cast-iron railings, sometimes with small balconies. The panelled front door had a fanlight that by this time had become semicircular, and was generally set between columns or pilasters supporting a curved or triangular pediment.

flights of fancy

By the beginning of the mid-Georgian period, the more ambitious architects had become bored by the constraints of Palladianism and were beginning to look further afield for inspiration. Some Palladian architects had been building exotic garden temples in the faux-medieval Gothick style, and these became particularly fashionable. In France, the rococo style, which was asymmetrical and very decorative, had become all the rage by this time. In Britain it was seen as exotic, frivolous and refreshing, and so it became a popular style for British interior architecture and furnishings.

An offshoot of rococo, chinoiserie – or 'the Chinese taste' – had also been trickling into Britain since the beginning of the century in the form of decorative accessories, furniture and fabrics. This taste for all things oriental began to affect architecture, too, initially in garden structures. Thanks to craftsmen like Thomas Chippendale, chinoiserie proliferated within the home until the end of the century.

neoclassicism

However, a passion for classical antiquities was at the heart of English architecture during the mid-Georgian period. While exteriors remained simple, interiors became more richly decorated. The leading exponent of this style, which eventually became known as neoclassicism, was Robert Adam. It was Adam who, with his brothers, changed the face of English domestic interiors. By drawing upon such sources as ancient Rome and Renaissance Italy, Adam extended the classical vocabulary with an array of decorative details, creating a style that was refined, elegant and innovative. It was applied not only to exteriors of houses but also to interiors, particularly plasterwork, fireplaces, furniture and accessories.

Towards the end of the century there was a move to strip neoclassicism of excessive ornamentation; a more 'chaste', crisp interpretation of Greek and Roman architecture became the ideal. Simultaneously, the Romanticism prevalent in the arts had led to the cult of the picturesque. This new Romantic sensibility and love of the exotic combined with the neo-Greek purism to produce Regency style – the culmination of neoclassicism.

The most adventurous and influential architect of this late Georgian period was John Nash, who was personal architect to the Prince Regent (later George IV). Taking inspiration from places as far afield as India and China, he was responsible for the extraordinary Brighton Pavilion, built for the hedonistic Prince. And as the result of his visionary civic planning, in London stuccoed facades enriched with fluted Greek columns or pilasters and wonderful ironwork gradually took precedence over the simple brick facades of the mid-Georgian period.

A more practical approach towards internal layout around this time saw the principal entertaining rooms beginning to be situated on the ground floor leading off a smaller hall. The staircase, which had previously been hidden, became an architectural feature leading grandly off the main hall and up to a central landing giving access to the principal bedrooms.

ABOVE: Modern craftsmanship is alive and well. The delicate, Georgian-style plasterwork shown in this over-door is from a new-build home in Atlanta, Georgia.

the early georgian interior

Georgian interiors were much more ornate and diverse than the elegantly understated exteriors. However, at the beginning of the Georgian era, Palladianism had a marked influence. The interiors of grand early Georgian houses were very 'architectural', with classical columns, pilasters, pediments and a heavy, dignified, austere formality. The walls were typically panelled from floor to ceiling, and a chair rail about a metre (three feet) above the floor ran between the upper and lower panels. The panelling was usually in an inexpensive wood such as deal (pine or fir), and so it was painted.

Gradually it became fashionable to use more plaster and less wood on walls. The wainscot, beneath the chair rail, was still panelled but above the chair rail the plaster wall was painted or hung with exotic textiles such as silk, velvet or damask, or the newly introduced flock wallpaper.

Walls and door frames were embellished with plain or fluted pilasters. Other decorative elements were carved from wood, as plaster moulds were not readily available. In grand houses the ceilings had large geometric panels enriched with robust mouldings and a deep cornice (cove). Humbler homes tended to have plain stuccoed or plastered ceilings, with the beams exposed or painted, and only a simple cornice.

The doors of main rooms generally had six panels, matching the wall panelling. In grand rooms, the doors were surrounded by a carved architrave surmounted by a pediment with carved details reflecting those of the cornice; the grandest homes had tall double doors.

BELOW: In a Georgian interior, doors and corridors would be lined up with through-views in mind. This is a view to a dining room from a drawing room on the other side of the hall. It is in a new-build home in Atlanta, Georgia.

OPPOSITE: The most richly decorated room in Chiswick House, the Blue Velvet Room was used by Lord Burlington as his study. Here is where visitors were shown his superb collection of architectural drawings by Palladio and Inigo Jones, who first introduced Palladio's work to England, in the 17th century. The spectacular ceiling is attributed to William Kent.

RIGHT: One of Robert Adam's signatures was his ceilings richly decorated with plasterwork motifs. Only this isn't an Adam ceiling, it is in the drawing room of a new-build country house in Scotland.

The fireplace and overmantel might be made in wood en suite with the panelling, but grand houses could have a marble surround. Carpets were rare, so most early Georgian reception rooms had polished deal boards. Furniture was arranged formally around the edge of a room.

the mid-georgian interior

By the middle of the eighteenth century it was fashionable for walls to be stuccoed or plastered, with a strong border below the cornice to frame the ceiling. Wood panelling on the wainscot began to disappear, and instead, the wall below the wooden chair rail would be marbled or painted in a flat white or stone shade. Above the chair rail it was painted or papered. Colours were strong, bright pastels.

Hand-painted Chinese papers were the height of fashion, as well as European chinoiserie papers mimicking them. Flock papers were still fashionable, and blockprinted papers with neoclassical decoration or *trompe l'oeil* architectural designs were also popular. In grand houses, elaborate ornamental plasterwork depicting classical swags, groups of trailing flowers or other classical motifs replaced pilasters as wall dividers and formed elaborate chimneybreasts complete with overmantels. The fireplace was now very much an independent feature, made in marble, stone or carved wood and decorated with neoclassical motifs – in fact, it was more like a piece of furniture and was often purchased like an antique.

Doors changed little, but their architraves and pediments began to reflect the more decorated style of the rooms. In grand houses the main rooms may have had mahogany doors with deep panelled reveals. More modest homes had doors of wood-grained or painted deal, often with Pompeian or Etruscan-style decoration.

Bare floorboards were still the norm, as carpets imported from Turkey and Persia remained expensive. However, rugs were now being made in England and were available for the wealthy. In the grandest houses, such as those by Adam, the design of the carpet often echoed that of the ceiling. These splendid ceilings had ornamental plaster mouldings that sometimes framed figurative painting.

the late georgian interior

The late Georgian period saw a return to much simpler interiors with more emphasis on comfort and entertaining. Carpets were now more widely available, and furniture was placed companionably in the centre of the rooms rather than arranged formally around the edge. Elaborate, layered window treatments and sometimes even tented ceilings added to the sense of comfort.

ABOVE: Pediments, a key feature of Palladian style, were used to emphasize doorways and entrances. They originated in ancient Greece, where they were used to crown the temples of the Greek gods.

ABOVE: The drawing room at Berrington Hall, Herefordshire, a house built in 1778–81 by Henry Holland, a pupil of Capability Brown. The imposing classical exterior gives way to a surprisingly delicate interior, with beautifully decorated ceilings and wonderful collections of Regency furniture.

There was little panelling on the walls, which were painted in any of a variety of finishes and incorporated strong, sharp colours such as acid yellow and crimson. Ceilings were much plainer, with a central rose or medallion and a decorated cornice with bold classical motifs as the main feature. Fireplaces continued to be a decorative feature but were simpler and flatter. All in all, interiors had become less showy, more comfortable and much more user-friendly.

OPPOSITE: This well-proportioned staircase is in an original 18th-century London town house. It is centred in the house, with a skylight above so that natural light filters from the top right down to the basement. The cantilevered stairs are made from stone, which could be cold, hard and noisy, so the custom-made carpet runner adds warmth and softness and deadens the sound. Note how the iron balusters on the principal floors give way to simple painted wood as the stairs rise to the attic. The mahogany handrail, typical of Georgian staircases, provides continuity and defines the dramatic outline.

RIGHT: This is the view from the entrance hall pictured overleaf, to the staircase shown opposite. The dramatic arch gracefully unites the two areas into one harmonious space. The mouldings are picked out in a subtle gold leaf which emphasizes the building's age and lends authenticity. The six-panelled door and over-door pediment are typical 18th-century features.

first impressions

In Georgian homes, the entrance hall was designed as a welcoming and impressive reception area, with the staircase a prominent architectural feature, leading to the principal rooms located up on the *piano nobile*. Although the halls were sparsely furnished initially, with full-height panelled walls, later developments saw plain walls with stronger colours, even wallpaper, and furniture grouped within the space so it would look more like a room than a passageway. Floors were typically stone, marble or wood – a practical tradition that has continued to this day.

welcoming space

I have two priorities when it comes to decorating a hall, whether in a traditional Georgian building or in a new house: practicality and a welcoming atmosphere. Country house halls with their generous proportions give you much more scope, including the possibility of installing a working fireplace with a seating area around it, which for me is the ultimate feature for a hall.

But no matter how tiny a hall may be, I will always try to furnish it as a room, even in a narrow town house where you have little more than a passage. I often cheat and cover a radiator with a casing to look like a piece of furniture and, if space permits, place chairs either side and a mirror above to reflect light. With a bit of clever planning a modest hallway can double as a dining area, a work space or a music room housing a piano.

The starting point for me in the hallway of the magnificent London town house shown here and on the previous spread was the subtle shade of pink of the original panelling. It just needed to be touched up and enhanced.

ABOVE: The ceiling in this hallway is, in fact, not panelled but painted with a *trompe l'oeil* finish to look like plaster panels. The paint is distressed and the cornice (cove) and mouldings are picked out in gold leaf.

LEFT: The drum table in the centre of the hall is furnished with coffee table books and a flower arrangement of hydrangeas. These touches make the area feel more like a room than a passageway.

OPPOSITE: The original panelling on the walls is painted in a two-tone dark salmon pink – a perfect, flattering shade for the gilt-framed paintings. The cast iron fireplace is probably a later addition, however. The original fireplace would have provided much-needed heat in the open space.

russian romance

Built just a few years ago by my good friends Rodney and Emily Cook (Rodney is an architect and designed the house himself, inspired by his love for England and his passion for Russia), this house is in a residential district of Atlanta. The inspiration for the architecture was based on a series of 'musts' that a Russian noble family should have had in their house – notably, a chapel, a library complete with scholarly books, and a grand setting that featured stables, follies and royal monuments. This house, which is set on raised ground, encapsulates all of the above and is a true romantic folly.

The main rooms at the front of the house are on the *piano nobile* and are approached by an external set of stone steps. This takes you to the ground floor and then you ascend up the grand spiral staircase to the main level. From the back of the house you enter straight into the hall at ground-floor level.

ABOVE LEFT, ABOVE AND OPPOSITE: The imposing staircase is sited in the centre of the house and forms the core from which the main rooms radiate. A series of thick plaster columns form the perimeter and support for the beautiful cantilevered wooden spiral staircase. The whole effect is more like a sculpture than a structural element. Symmetrical arches lead off the hall to the drawing room, dining room and kitchen, and because there are no doors you get really interesting views from a variety of angles through these arches back to the staircase. The architectural cornice which runs in this space and into the drawing room was inspired by a similar one from the Parthenon, although, of course, this is much smaller in scale.

fine detail

Built on a stunning, secluded 18-acre site in Atlanta, this Georgian-style new-build house is the epitome of class, craftsmanship and everything that is reminiscent of the best of eighteenth-century culture. The talented architect was Les Cole from Alabama, and we worked together closely on every detail, from the layout and flow of the rooms, the plasterwork, cornicing and panelling down to the lighting and finishes, to ensure that the client was happy before the building works commenced.

Built from Texas limestone, the house blends into the mature landscape with a grandeur that is, in the true spirit of the eighteenth century, far from ostentatious. Unusually for American-built homes, the entire structure, including the walls, is solid

ABOVE LEFT: The main front door is unusual in that it is not solid but glazed. It was designed to benefit from the double aspect of the hall and views through to the garden. The over-door broken pediment is supported by corbels and a carved frieze to emphasize its importance.

ABOVE: A Regency mahogany marble-top pier table with a mirrored back sits perfectly in the void under the staircase. The picture above it is actually set into a recess and revolves within the frame, giving you a choice of pictures to admire.

ABOVE: A large mahogany side table flanked by two high-back upholstered armchairs makes a lovely grouping opposite the staircase. The bright oil painting adds colour to the otherwise very clean and architectural hall.

rather than wood-frame, which is definitely noticeable once inside. The main entrance, which is accessed from the garden side, tends to be used only when entertaining formally, so it is rarely used by the family. The hall itself, however, is regularly walked through, as it leads from the kitchen and family room to the main living room and main bedroom on the same floor.

The staircase, which leads from ground to first floor, is built in limestone and cantilevered to make the most of the proportions and the general open-plan feel of the house. The beautiful wrought-iron balusters are highlighted in gold leaf. A half-landing has a large picture window overlooking the back garden with stunning views towards a cascade of water steps.

LEFT: The floor of the hall in this Las Vegas house is a traditional limestone with insets of black marble and a matching border set in from the edge of the room to define the area. The mahogany double doors with the arched fanlight are a typical feature of the eighteenth century. As the ceiling height was good, a chair rail with wainscot panelling below was installed as a traditional feature and to make the most of the generous proportions. The use of antique furniture and traditional brass lanterns helps to create a welcoming atmosphere.

OPPOSITE TOP: The view from the hall looking towards the drawing room is framed with an arch. Because American homes tend to be much more open-plan than traditional English houses, there is more light and depth to work with. The yellow wallpaper connects one space to another.

OPPOSITE BOTTOM: This antique mahogany side table with its richly carved frieze and the landscape painting above create a focal point and anchor the space, making the hallway feel like a room rather than a corridor.

an oasis in las vegas

You would never know, on entering this hall, that you were in the bustling heart of Las Vegas, a city where day and night are as one – you could easily be tucked away in the English countryside. My clients, who are both passionate about the Georgian period, wanted to create a little oasis to escape from life in the fast lane.

The style of this home is similar to a Palladian villa. The house was designed by the Atlanta-based architect William Baker. He and I worked closely on the internal layouts and architectural features, starting with the most essential – great proportions. These applied not only to room sizes, but to the height and width of doors and windows, the scale and details of cornices, and all the other architectural features. The entrance to the house is up a double flight of external stairs, so the main rooms are essentially on the *piano nobile*. As first impressions are all-important, it was essential to create a welcoming yet impressive space to set the tone for the rest of the house.

contemporary craftsmanship

ABOVE: The Tuscan columns in the huge hall of this Scottish house are not, in fact, structural but they visually anchor the large beam above them. The windows in the two-storey wall allow the light to flood in.

ABOVE RIGHT: Detail of the edge of the mahogany staircase in the hall, which was designed by Mark Hopton. Note that each tread has three different styles of turned baluster.

OPPOSITE: The staircase was inspired by one that my client had seen in an original Georgian home. It is an exemplary example of interior architecture and craftsmanship.

It is hard to believe that this magnificent house is barely a year old. I wish I could be around in three hundred years' time to see it still standing in all its glory. The location is stunning, on the edge of a beautiful Scottish river – even the most talented of artists would be hard put to conjure up a more spectacular setting.

This house was built to last. Designed by the Edinburgh-based firm LDN Architects (formerly Law & Dunbar-Naismith), it evolved with the guidance of the conservation architect Mark Hopton, who incorporated my clients' clear and imaginative design ideas. The beauty of a project like this is the chance to be involved from the beginning, and to have a blank canvas and talented craftsmen from which to create a dream home. We are so fortunate to have craftsmen with the skills and ability to create homes that are the equal of those built during the eighteenth century.

ABOVE: A view of the magnificent plaster ceiling and one of the two specially commissioned chandeliers in the hall.

ABOVE TOP RIGHT: Detail showing the finely moulded flowers, foliage and fruit in each corner of the plasterwork ceiling.

ABOVE BOTTOM RIGHT: Doves perch among the flowers in the capital of each column in the upper floor. The plaster ceiling hides its structural strength: the main support beam that divides the two areas of the hall is dressed with the same plaster cornice to make it an integral part of the ceiling.

OPPOSITE: The fireplace, made from English stone, was custom-made for the space. The fine carved frieze depicts a hunting scene from the local landscape. The floor is of pine imported from America, and the central inset, which reflects the circle in the plasterwork above, has a circular marquetry pattern depicting Scottish flora and fauna.

The plasterwork ceiling of the hall is a true work of art, inspired by a ceiling that came from a municipal building in the north of England. The intention was to use the original plasterwork, but the size was not quite right and the work to restore it and make it fit the space was just not practical. This masterpiece was executed by Hayles & Howe, who created hundreds of new moulds so that each section is unique. The swags over the fireplace and to either side of it were the inspiration of my client and were hand-applied after the walls had been given a specialist paint finish.

I had the two massive chandeliers specially made for the space. Their design was inspired by a chandelier that came from Easton Neston, a grand country house in Northamptonshire. Cleverly executed by Dernier & Hamlyn to incorporate spotlights that highlight the walls and intricate details of the plasterwork ceiling, they have a classic yet contemporary feel.

living rooms

The Georgians were quite specific in naming their living spaces. Drawing rooms were large and formal and meant to impress. Sitting rooms, altogether smaller and more intimate, were for gatherings of family and close friends. And studies were places to catch up privately on correspondence or maybe become absorbed in a novel. In today's home we can add family rooms, media rooms and dens to the list.

ABOVE: In this new-build house in Las Vegas, the deep, panelled window reveals are similar to those found in Georgian houses. The floor is oak plank and adds a warm feel to the room, as do the piano and antique furniture.

LEFT: Although it is a walk-through open-plan space, this large, sun-filled drawing room has the typical proportions and furnishings of a Georgian country house.

a flowing space

In many older houses, the drawing room is often too large and too formal and is situated away from the hub of the house, which means that it ends up a bit forgotten and infrequently used. The advantage of building a house from scratch is that you can arrange it as you like, especially when planning the flow of the rooms.

The drawing room shown here, on the previous spread and overleaf, although used as a formal entertaining space, is welcoming and serene. It is located directly off the hall (pictured on pages 26–7), and because you need to walk through it to get anywhere, it is part of the daily life of the house and is regularly used to play the piano and to access the terrace that overlooks the back garden. In essence the layout has done away with any need for a dark corridor, which can be wasted space.

With typical Georgian proportions and three tall French doors, the room naturally divides into two seating areas, one focused around the fireplace and the other against the opposite wall. The pale lemon colour of the walls is repeated in the silk curtains, which are deliberately left simple so as not to detract from the view. The starting point for the colour scheme was the muted tones of the reproduction Aubusson rug.

RIGHT: The light-filled drawing room is on the way to everywhere in the house. Three French doors surmounted by arched windows lead directly out to a terrace. Simple Venetian-style curtains follow the line of the arches and largely remain open as the room is not overlooked.

LEFT: A silk check fabric complements the pink and green small woven floral design used to upholster a pair of *bergère* armchairs. It is fine to mix patterns together in one room as long as the patterns complement each other in terms of colour and scale, as they do here.

OPPOSITE: This reproduction French *fauteuil* is covered in a beautiful silk brocade and trimmed with a gimp braid rather than studs, which would have been too heavy for the fabric.

RIGHT: A detail showing the back of the *fauteuil*. A contrast fabric such as a check is often used for the backs of such chairs, but in this case we have used the same fabric all over, so that the chairs are completely at one with the lovely Aubusson-style rug.

restoring the glory

ABOVE: The room is naturally divided into two seating areas, defined by the rugs and a pair of beautiful crystal chandeliers. The colour scheme of blues and creams runs through both areas.

LEFT: View of the south-west corner, which has the seating area defined by a beautiful Persian silk carpet. The outer curtains and swagged pelmets are in a custom-made woven fabric – secondary curtains in silk sit behind and can be drawn at night. The contemporary sculpture adds a focal point to the corner.

This classic double drawing room is in the original Palladian wing of an English country house. Situated on the *piano nobile*, it benefits from southerly and westerly views and plenty of sunlight. The house had been uninhabited for many years, so it required a comprehensive renovation. The brief from my clients was to retain as many of the original architectural features and as much of the character as possible while making a practical, twenty-first century home. In this room, the mouldings on the ceiling and the chair rail were added, but the pilasters dividing the two areas are original. The wood parquet floor is new – the waxed finish gives it a lovely, authentic patina. The walls above the chair rail are upholstered in a cream linen fabric and below they are painted with a stippled, glazed finish. The combination of modern and antique furniture and art gives any room a classic, contemporary feel.

OPPOSITE: An antique bureau sits in the recess to one side of the fireplace. It makes a perfect working area and a useful surface on which to set lamps and display decorative objects. I prefer to use antique pieces rather than built-in furniture in recesses unless storage space is needed.

BELOW: The view from the original, extremely elegant floor-to-ceiling large-paned windows is towards the green oasis of the communal gardens. The room has wall-to-wall carpet, but the seating area around the fireplace is defined by an antique rug.

townhouse elegance

The drawing room in the London town house pictured here and on pages 42–5 occupies the whole of the first floor and so it has a double aspect, making it light and sunny all day. In eighteenth-century houses the grander entertaining rooms were always placed on the first floor, or *piano nobile*, and given proportions to match – high ceilings and tall windows. With big windows like these I prefer to use a plain fabric that will not dominate the room. The pelmets are enhanced by carved, gilded pelmets inspired by those used in the Georgian period.

Often these grand old rooms have two doorways, in which case it may be a good idea to block up one of them in order to create more wall space for furniture and paintings (provided, of course, there are no building regulations preventing this).

The drawing room is divided into three seating areas, with the fireplaces providing the main focal points. The fire surrounds are not original – they were no doubt sold or changed by previous owners – but I found replacements in a style that is correct for the room. Antique furniture and pictures add warmth and a contrast for the pale upholstery.

The drawing room does not have a chair rail or panelling, so the walls are painted in a pale, dragged finish consistent with its atmosphere of graceful age. The woodwork is painted and distressed in a light cream colour, which is less harsh than bright white. The room is lit by indirect lighting, a pair of chandeliers and matching wall sconces and lamps. This provides a much softer ambient light than spots or downlights, which would be inappropriate here.

OPPOSITE: An elegant 18th-century settee with a painted and gilded frame is flanked by boxed-in radiators which could not be placed under the windows (my preferred choice). The original chinoiserie painted panels are in keeping with the scheme of the room and are more delicate than one large painting.

BELOW: A classic sofa table is used to divide the space between the two main seating areas – much more attractive than seeing the back of a sofa. It also provides space for an additional light source. When planning your room, remember to add floor sockets in strategic positions.

LEFT: This antique chest of drawers is displayed with a collection of antique chinoiserie objects. Mahogany was one of the most widely used woods for furniture of the Georgian area, having been introduced in the 1720s. Early pieces were simple with elegant proportions.

OPPOSITE: The secondary seating area, which faces south. Once again the furniture placement is arranged around a fireplace, and the new, custom-made club fender gives additional seating. The gilt *fauteuils* are antique but have been reupholstered in a brocade fabric. The rug is an antique Aubusson.

a venetian window

The drawing room on the *piano nobile* of a traditional Georgian town house, pictured here and overleaf, is graced by a Venetian window, a typical feature of Palladian architecture. The central section of the window has a semi-circular top and is flanked by two narrow windows, the tops of which should align with the spring of the central window arch.

Venetian windows are tricky to dress with curtains. The key is to retain the shape of the arch and not hide too many of the architectural features, while softening the overall effect. The solution here was to add a carved, gilded pelmet, which makes a perfect frame from which to hang a swagged pelmet. Plain fabrics such as silks, damasks and velvets are appropriate for the window treatments of formal rooms, and all were traditionally employed in the eighteenth century.

The walls are panelled with the original mouldings, picked out in three tones of yellow. This room is fortunate to have survived with all the original features intact, apart from the fireplace, which is a copy of an eighteenth-century marble surround.

LEFT: The room, though well proportioned, was not large enough to split into two seating areas, so it was natural for the fireplace to become the main focal point, and this comfortable, elegant sofa forms part of that seating group.

RIGHT: This *trompe l'oeil* painted panel has been hand-applied to the ceiling and picked out in subtle colours to enhance the design. Light gilding adds to the grandeur of this elegant drawing room.

BELOW: The egg-and-dart moulding is original. It is actually plaster but, typically, and more often today, the mouldings are made from wood and applied into the panels. By painting the mouldings and then wiping them back to expose the white base coat, more emphasis is given to the details. The white Carrara marble fireplace is reproduction but copied from an original 18th-century design.

BELOW RIGHT: Detail showing the relationship between the chair rail, wall and panels and how they sit with the reeded door architrave. The painted door is original and has egg-and-dart moulding in the fielded panels. The Georgians left nothing to chance and every detail was planned and executed with utmost precision, leaving us wonderful examples of craftsmanship to follow today.

LEFT: Although it is in a London town house, this family living room has a country feel, largely due to the use of country-style materials such as the carved pine fireplace, wood plank floor and country furniture. It doubles as a dining area and is open-plan to the kitchen, so this informal feel is quite appropriate.

BELOW: The television is cleverly disguised in this custom-made piece of furniture, which looks like an oak chest of drawers when closed.

family room

Today's living lends itself to having one large space where the family members, whatever their ages, can congregate and spend their limited free time together, eating, watching television, playing games and cooking. Many new homes already have such a multi-function space, but when renovating a traditional house this general family area is more difficult to achieve. The house may be listed as a historic gem, which limits the walls you can knock down and the location of services. In this town house the kitchen and dining area have been successfully combined by creating a large opening between the two, leaving the option to convert back to the original layout should circumstances or needs change.

OPPOSITE: A comfortable sofa makes the room multi-functional, which is especially important with a young family. The large 19th-century gilt mirror is an antique shop find that helps give the room more depth and reflected light. The painted corner cupboard is probably French and provides useful storage for toys and china, as well as a nice contrast to all the natural wood.

regency style

The beautifully proportioned drawing room pictured here and on pages 54–7 is typical of many London town houses, where the main entertaining room is situated on the *piano nobile* and is double-aspect. More Regency in style, this room has floor-to-ceiling sash windows with large panes and narrow glazing bars – glazing bars became increasingly attenuated as the eighteenth century progressed.

Rooms with this layout generally lend themselves to two seating areas focused around the two fireplaces. In this case the fireplace in the smaller, somewhat narrow area at one end had been removed, allowing a cosy secondary seating area to be created which would have been difficult had the fireplace remained. One of the two entrance doors was also removed, allowing a more practical placement of the furniture (two armchairs instead of one) in the main area.

The wood parquet floor laid in a traditional herringbone pattern is new – the original flooring was wood plank. In my view the herringbone is more elegant for this style of room and provides a great background for the fine Persian silk rugs. The walls are wallpapered in a pale blue-grey ragged effect, which could also have been achieved using a specialist paint finish.

The curtains are in a contemporary damask and the trimmings hand-made to complement the fabric. Although there are many standard trimmings available, it is sometimes easier and more economical to have one specially commissioned, with matching tassel tiebacks. In this way you can ensure the proportions and colours are just right.

LEFT: A combination of antique and reproduction furniture was used for this room, an approach that works very well here, especially because items such as coffee tables are, of course, impossible to find as genuine antique pieces.

OPPOSITE: Although not original to the house, the fireplace is antique and in keeping, being Regency in style. It is made from white Carrara marble and has an inset register grate, in this case with a gas coal fire. The French antique *fauteuils* are probably late 19th-century copies of 18th-century originals, but their antique gilded finish is perfect for the elegant and subtle room decor. The mirror is a continental repoussé mirror with a bevelled plate, in a fine carved gilded frame – the proportions are perfect for the room.

BELOW: Details of the carving on one of the French antique *fauteuils*. The brocade fabric is trimmed with gimp to hide the nails, which is more discreet than using studs.

ABOVE: A simple fresh flower arrangement can add colour and life to an elegant room. Where possible use flowers that are in season and echo the colours of the room.

ABOVE AND OPPOSITE: The damask curtains in this London town house are traditionally designed with swags and tails (cascades) to suit the proportions of the room and frame the windows elegantly. It is important to get the proportion correct for swags and tails – typically the deepest part of the swag is approximately one fifth the length of the curtain, and the tails fall about half to two thirds of the way down the curtains. I tend to look at each window treatment in situ to judge the optimum length and depth of the swag and tails. The back of the swag should be lined in a contrast fabric rather than a basic curtain lining. The tassel fringe has a braided top rather than a cord, which makes it more flexible and easier to follow the folds of the swag.

RIGHT: The rope cord with single tassel tieback was specially commissioned, picking out the colours of the furnishings.

oriental cinema

This media room on the third floor of a London town house is designed for the family to watch big-screen films. The style is oriental/Ottoman, which is reflected in the furnishings and the accessories. The vibrant colours reflect those of a theatre and are highly suitable for a room largely used at night or when darkened to optimize the quality of the screen. The room already had the chair rail installed, so the walls above and below were painted in tones of yellow picked to blend with the fabrics. Wall-to-wall carpet helps with the acoustics of the room, which has surround-sound speakers concealed within the built-in cabinets.

TOP: The specially commissioned lampshade reflects the oriental theme of the room. The colours of the shade and trim are taken from the other fabrics used in the room.

ABOVE: The Ottoman-style bolsters divide the seating into individual spaces and at the same time provide armrests.

TOP: This pretty silk lampshade is trimmed with red and clear glass beads.

ABOVE: Following the Ottoman theme, the stool holds a tray of Turkish tea glasses along with a silver teapot.

the ultimate den

Situated on the lower ground floor of a new-build house in Las Vegas, this versatile room is a multi-functional space where young and old can meet or entertain family and friends. The floor is travertine, which on its own could be cold, but with the oak beam ceiling and wood panelling below the chair rail and the green-painted walls, the effect is both welcoming and practical. Because the room leads to the outside and a covered veranda, it was essential to have a floor surface that was practical for children running in and out from the pool, and one that would visually unite the two areas when the doors were open.

The area around the stone open fireplace is used primarily for television viewing, and the television is concealed in the custom-built unit to the right of the fireplace.

ABOVE: This is a room designed for fun and relaxation. There's a large, squashy sofa to collapse on and watch television, a table for card games or snacks, and a serious billiard table with plenty of room around it to line up the shots.

ABOVE RIGHT: The clubhouse feel of the room is reinforced by the wood panelling, the dark green walls and the invitingly scuffed leather sofa.

With chairs and a strategically placed overhead light, the country oak table is predominantly an area for playing card games or board games but is also used by the children as somewhere to gather for a light snack. The back part of the room, which leads to the wine cellar, is the ideal place for the billiard table. The light above it is custom-made.

With little surface area for lamps, wall sconces are invaluable, providing useful additional light – in this case the candle bulbs are exposed, creating a traditional look, but shades could be used for a softer light. The rug and tartan curtains help with sound absorption, and the old leather sofa gives the room a comfortable, casual, masculine feel.

luminous room with a view

This beautifully proportioned upstairs drawing room has stunning views over natural landscape, despite being in the heart of the busy city of Atlanta. The room runs the full width of the house and has a triple aspect, which makes it beautifully light but leaves little wall space for furniture. However, the clever choice and placement of the pieces allow for two main seating groups with plenty of space in the centre for guests to mingle and enjoy pre-dinner drinks.

The antique Persian rug provides most of the colour in the room, and the windows are simply dressed with swagged draperies that do not detract from the view. The pale grey walls are a classical colour – a good neutral background for the artwork.

OPPOSITE: The two daughters of the house regularly use the grand piano, the top of which is crammed with photographs of friends and family. The family portrait adds a contemporary touch and a big splash of colour. It came from their previous home and is slightly too tall for this room, so has to sit over the chair rail and also overlap the cornice (cove).

RIGHT: The fireplace was inspired by a temple, the Erechtheion, on the Acropolis in Athens. It features two caryatids (draped female figures used as columns) copied from those supporting the temple's Porch of the Maidens. They are positioned to look as though they are turning outwards to greet guests entering the room. The fireplace is flanked by a pair of antique wing chairs that belonged to the owner's grandmother. The pictures are by several American Luminist painters.

inspired by a persian-style rug

The elegant and calm family sitting room shown here was designed by my good friend Patricia McLean, a talented designer based in Atlanta. The house is in one of the pretty tree-laden areas of the city, with this room looking over the beautiful tiered landscaped garden, and the tranquillity of the beautiful setting creates the impression of being deep in the countryside. The previous owners had added the architectural arches to the French doors and the wooden fireplace.

I often take my inspiration for the decoration of a room from a single item, such as a lovely faded Aubusson rug, a painting or a particularly striking fabric. Here, the colours were inspired by the reproduction Persian-style rug, and the printed fabric was selected to give a relaxed country feel, while ensuring the colours tied in with the adjacent rooms. The antique Regency-style club chairs and small chest of drawers between the armchairs add character and depth to the room.

RIGHT: The botanical prints above the imposing fireplace are fixed to an ingenious screen that folds back to reveal a flat-screen television. Floor-to-ceiling French doors open directly onto a terrace, allowing easy transition between the cool interior and the hot Atlanta summers.

BELOW: The sky blue walls that the owner had loved in her previous home are used here in a flat paint finish that beautifully contrasts with the yellows and reds of the upholstery.

The colours of the living room, also designed by Patricia McLean, were inspired by the framed, hand-painted Chinese wall panels by De Gournay, a company specializing in magnificent eighteenth-century chinoiserie designs. The predominantly blue and cream colour scheme was selected to give a cool, serene atmosphere,

LEFT: It is very much in the American tradition for rooms to open into one another without intervening corridors. With the doors open, it gives the house an enviably cool, open-plan feeling. The blue and cream check on the upholstered armchair pulls together the walls and curtains, giving a more contemporary feel.

BELOW: A pair of antique upright armchairs flank the fireplace in the secondary seating area. They are upholstered in a bright red moiré that exactly matches the red leaves in the chinoiserie panel, adding a real zing to the scheme.

with a more formal feel than the family room. The owners had used the blue paint colour on the walls in their previous house and rightly assumed it was a great colour for displaying their artwork and their antique porcelain and accessories.

RIGHT: Another little touch of chinoiserie, in the shape of a table lamp base inspired by a Chinese ginger jar. This detail also shows how different patterns, in this case a check, a floral print and a stripe, can work together in harmony if colour and scale are taken into consideration.

BELOW: The antique French-painted gilded mirror is the perfect harmonious counterpoint for the Chinese panels. The gilding is soft and slightly distressed – there's not a harsh note in the entire room.

living rooms

BELOW: This beautifully proportioned double-aspect drawing room is in a newly built home in a US city. The ceilings are 4.3 metres (14 feet) high, and the six full-height French doors allow stunning views of the garden. As in many American houses, there are no internal doors closing off the room, so a large opening with a plastered, fan-arched top is placed at each corner of the room, for balance and symmetry. The main seating area, which is emphasized by a large reproduction rug, is arranged around the fireplace.

OPPOSITE TOP: An antique mahogany bookcase with glazed top forms the focal point of the wall opposite the fireplace. This stunning piece of furniture draws the eye upwards, emphasising the height of the ceilings. It is flanked by a pair of upholstered mahogany library chairs. The bookcase provides a useful display cabinet for antique porcelain.

BELOW RIGHT: The marble fire surround was an antique piece purchased in England and it forms the main focal point in the room. The applied wall panelling helps divide the large height of the walls but it is important to keep the panels large enough to accommodate pictures. The walls are dragged in a pale gold that is the same tone as the silk curtains. The pretty ormolu candelabras add authenticity to this room in the style of the 18th century.

scottish symmetry

This supremely elegant yet welcoming drawing room is in a newly built house, and yet walking into the room you would never believe it. The details, scale and proportion are as good as in any genuine eighteenth-century mansion, and the superb craftsmanship speaks for itself. Naturally divided into two main seating areas grouped around the two fireplaces, and a third in front of the large bow window that sits between them both, it was an easy room to furnish. The ceiling is 4.3 metres (14 feet) high, so it made sense to install a chair rail and use separate wall treatments above and below it.

Two chandeliers are placed centrally over the main seating areas. Although they have large ceiling roses to anchor them, the remainder of the ceiling would have felt bare without additional panel moulding, which we designed and executed

BELOW LEFT: One of the two custom-made fireplaces. Although they are very similar, each has its own unique details. A sofa table sits behind the large, three-seater sofa and provides a good divider between the two areas. Floor sockets were strategically placed in the middle of this room so a lamp can be used on this table without trailing cables.

BELOW: A view showing the fine architectural details of the ceiling, door frames and over-door pediment. The curtains are in the same silk as the wall covering and have matching swags and tails (cascades).

BELOW: A view towards one end of the drawing room which shows the three seating areas defined by area rugs. The walls have a silk damask fabric above the chair rail, and below the rail is a painted, lightly stippled finish in a slightly darker colour. Natural light floods through the floor-to-ceiling windows, which frame a fantastic panoramic view. Indirect artificial light comes from the two chandeliers, strategically placed lamps and picture lights.

with Hayles & Howe. This, however, did create a small challenge, as the fireplaces do not sit exactly centrally on the two end walls because of two doorways leading to other rooms.

It was obvious to me that we needed to create an oblong space centrally in the room and plan the ceiling layout symmetrically around it, even though it meant that the chandeliers were not quite in line with the fireplaces. The ceiling was left in one colour here, but for added emphasis you could add a light touch of gilding. (It is worth remembering that, generally speaking, the chandelier should be placed centrally in a room rather than in relation to the furniture layout. The one exception is the dining room, where it may be better to hang a chandelier centrally over the table.) The ceiling in the bay, which is lower, was deliberately left plain.

ABOVE AND ABOVE RIGHT: A garden room in the newly built Scottish country house shown on the previous spread. The exposed stone wall looks as if it had been in place since medieval times, but it's another example of modern craftsmanship at its best. Massively tall wooden sash windows flood the place with light and sunshine (the Scottish climate permitting) and the furniture is suitably rustic: solid pine, wicker and comfortable, tartan-upholstered chairs. A perfect spot to laze away a sunny Sunday morning with the newspapers.

OPPOSITE: This chinoiserie-style room is situated at the end of a corridor, making this area something of a passage or lobby (it leads to a library on the right and another sitting room on the left) but it has been treated and furnished as a room. The hand-painted wallpaper by De Gournay was made in panels to fit, so each wall was carefully planned to take account of doorways, fireplace, etc. The coral and black colour scheme is oriental in nature, and the furniture is Chinese black lacquer. Woodwork and plasterwork have been subtly aged and picked out with black and gilt, keeping the theme consistent throughout the room. The cornice was specially made with a deep cove decorated with bamboo and birds. The fans in the corners are another detail of the chinoiserie theme, which was very popular in the mid- to late 18th century.

ABOVE LEFT: This drawing room on the *piano nobile* of an 18th-century London town house is fairly typical of London's Georgian town houses. However, this one retains many of its original features, such as the panelled window and window seat reveal. A pair of George III armchairs and a skirted table form a conversation area for two. The antique wall sconces, now electrified, would originally have been used with candles.

LEFT: The Regency style fireplace is antique marble and was purchased from a dealer in London. The tiles are original from the 1890s and came from Thomas Elsley.

RIGHT: The floor is wood plank and, although new, is reminiscent of what would have been there. The duck-egg blue walls are an early Georgian colour chosen to tie in with the Mahal rug. The silk festoon curtain, also appropriate for the period, frames the windows and cuts out far less light and space than individual pairs of curtains.

sun protection

This pretty Scandinavian Gustavian-style conservatory is adjacent to a London kitchen, providing a link between the interior and the garden as well as a comfortable, sunny area for relaxing and reading. The stone floor has been covered with a neutral wool carpet to provide a softer surface for young children. The simple roof shades offer protection from the strong rays and help prevent the furnishing fabrics from fading. Roller shades are also used for these south-facing windows. People often underestimate how hot a south-facing conservatory can be, even in northern climates. It is important to establish a good through-draught.

OPPOSITE: The painted furniture and mirrors are old pieces found in a variety of modest antique shops. In a room that leads outdoors, it is important to keep the style simple and neutral and not to detract from nature with anything too formal or with brightly coloured schemes.

RIGHT: In winter the shades are rolled back to make the most of the winter sun, and that is the time when heat is required. The radiator covers in this conservatory have wood grilles which are reminiscent of garden planters or old-fashioned wood-burning stoves.

home offices
and libraries

The concept of a home library was developed in the eighteenth century. Beautifully illustrated and bound books were being printed in Britain for the first time, and well-to-do gentlemen travelling through Europe on the Grand Tour were acquiring both books and artefacts to bring home. They needed space to display them and a place to retreat into their scholarly world. Today, libraries and studies should offer a cosy alternative to the sitting room or the kitchen table and provide a practical place to work and play.

LEFT: This basement home office is an eclectic mixture of traditional and modern. Although it has a window, natural daylight is limited, so the vivid blue walls enhance the space. The bookcases were custom-made to look more like furniture than built-ins. The floor is oak planks and the fireplace is a marble reproduction with inset gas fire. The contemporary art over the fireplace, although probably too large for the fire surround, effectively breaks up the expanse of blue wall.

original features

From the late eighteenth century, architects were designing homes with separate rooms to house collections of books. They incorporated either built-in shelving or, more typically, large, free-standing mahogany bookcases with a glazed upper section and cupboards below. Specific library furniture developed alongside the room, such as desks, folio and reading stands, library steps, caned armchairs with leather seats and drum tables. Originally, the decoration was dark, largely because it went with the dark furniture and provided a good background colour for displaying artefacts.

The library shown here benefits from the original, beautifully proportioned panelling of an eighteenth-century town house. The walls are picked out in tones of green and warm beige that enhance and give added depth to the fielded panels. The fireplace is simple marble but probably not original to the room. The floor-to-ceiling French doors open onto little balconies and help bring some daylight into a fairly dark room on the *piano nobile*. The panelled reveals are working shutters, a nice architectural feature and useful from a security point of view.

OPPOSITE: The curtains were chosen to give warmth and a dash of masculine, Regency atmosphere. The gilded pelmets were traditionally used during the 18th century to provide a clear break between the window and the cornice (cove), just as they do here. The room, which houses a harp and a harpsichord, doubles as a music room.

ABOVE RIGHT: A detail showing how a radiator casing has been cleverly matched in with the chair rail and panelling. Fine paint effects were used to enhance the different areas and types of mouldings.

RIGHT: The built-in bookcase is an integral part of this panelled room and is beautifully constructed to work in terms of proportion and also as a functional piece. Traditional libraries look so much better if leather-bound books are on display and the more functional titles stored in the cupboards below. The reproduction wing chair is a comfy place to curl up and read.

ABOVE: This panelled library is a mere eight years old, yet you would think it had been maturing its look for centuries. Here, one of two brass hurricane wall lights that frame one of the built-in bookcases throws soft light onto the rich mahogany panelling with its carved bead moulding.

RIGHT: The panelling is a beautiful flame mahogany which is also used for the doors. Bookcases are incorporated around two sides of the room, and on this wall a gap is left for the sofa and two swing-arm reading lamps. The ceiling is plaster with a grid of mahogany panel mouldings, while the floor is traditional oak, with a pale area rug adding light and warmth. The two full-length French doors open onto a beautiful terrace, and the windows are dressed in a horizontally striped chenille velvet.

a practical space

Moving into the nineteenth century, the library became more of a family room – a place to play games, read and sit comfortably by the fire – and furnishings changed accordingly. Comfortable sofas and chairs replaced hard, upright library chairs. Wallpapers and bright colours ousted the early Georgian dark green and red walls, and built-in wooden book-cases were painted.

Today, a happy medium lies somewhere between the heavy panelling and the patterned wallpaper – a room that is light and inviting, conducive to study or work, with uplifting splashes of colour coming from rugs, books and furniture fabrics. Before deciding on the exact layout, first establish how the room will be used and by whom; will a free-standing desk be required or would it be a better use of the space to build one in? Will a television be wanted, and should it be hidden or exposed? In town houses and smaller rooms, I prefer painted bookshelves (not necessarily white), but in the country it is perhaps more appropriate to use natural wood and continue the theme into panelling.

LEFT: A good-looking town house study with smart striped walls, free-standing floor-to-ceiling bookcases and a working fireplace, with the original late 17th-century tiles. Note the practical library step and the leather-topped desk.

OPPOSITE: The garden end of the library in a newly built Georgian-style country house. This is a magnificent example of panelling, which would be the envy of the best 18th-century craftsmen. All the elements are in place here: chairs that would not look out of place in a gentlemen's club, a lovely faded antique rug and a splash of exuberance in the practical roller shades.

dining rooms

Georgian dining rooms had a masculine feel

to them, as often the men dined alone or the

ladies retreated as soon as the meal was over.

Decorative themes included anything to do with

wine or hunting, and walls were covered with

either fabric or, in grand houses, tapestries.

Candlelight was essential, so side tables and

mantelpieces were adorned with candelabras,

which were often set in front of mirrors for

reflected light. The effect would have been very

atmospheric and theatrical – which is just what a

formal dining room should be today.

LEFT: This pretty blue dining room, designed by Patricia McLean from Atlanta, leads off the main entrance and onto the garden beyond, giving a great vista from the front door. When not in use for congenial dining, the table is used to display a beautiful flower arrangement and coffee table books. The room is almost square, so a round table works best – visually, it is anchored by the rug below and the chandelier above.

OPPOSITE: With the wonderful panelling to live up to, furnishing this dining room required careful attention to detail. The chairs were bought at auction, the seats were recovered and the 18th-century-style table with two pedestals and leaves was made to fit the room. The sideboard is also 18th-century and the rug is a fine Persian silk carpet.

LEFT: It is difficult to place radiators against panelled walls, and they tend to ruin the proportions of a wall. This one is cleverly disguised inside a specially commissioned wrought iron, marble-topped radiator case, with details picked out in gilt. It doubles as a useful additional shelf for displaying artefacts or serving food.

a classic refreshed

This classical dining room in an eighteenth-century London town house is blessed with its original Georgian panelling – it's a style that is widely copied and used in many a room today. The original colour of the panels was not dissimilar to what is there now, but it was a little tired and drab, so specialist painters gave it an updated look using combinations of tints taken from the fabric.

This room is used mainly at night, so candlelight from the two sets of candelabras and two pairs of wall sconces provide most of the light. It does have a pretty view over the garden, so the colours of the curtains were selected to blend with the outside. Shades offer privacy and help to protect the fabrics and artwork.

a shimmer of gold dust

Situated in a house in the heart of London, this well-proportioned dining room leads off the narrow entrance. In order to make the space feel larger we installed double doors, making the two spaces became one and allowing more natural daylight to flow into the hall. The floors throughout the house were new, and fine herringbone parquet was used to replace the original wood planks. This, in fact, worked well with the scale and style of the rooms. The existing marble fireplace was cleaned and restored and a new, efficient gas fire was added.

The walls are painted in a specialist paint finish: a soft rag roll with gold dust added to the glaze to make them shimmer and reflect the light. The curtains are in contemporary-style silk damask with the tails contrast-lined in a shimmering gold silk and edged with a custom-made fringe.

RIGHT: The table and chairs were custom-made for the room, the chandelier is an antique and the original fireplace is of white Carrara marble.

BELOW: Coloured glass adds sparkle and a nice contrast to the dark mahogany wood. When used for dinner parties, white linen mats protect the table, as well as breaking up the expanse of wood to give a more formal feel.

sophisticated plum

Designed mainly for use at night, the dining room pictured here and overleaf is painted in a beautiful red plum colour – perfect for sophisticated dinner parties. It is one of a series of beautifully proportioned rooms in a newly built home in the United States, but it has the feel of an authentic Regency dining room.

The Venetian curtains in plum and gold brocade – colours suggested by the antique rug, which was the starting point for the colour scheme – follow the line of the arched windows. A gilt-wood mirror hangs between the windows to reflect light from the chandelier.

The table and chairs are custom-made from mahogany. It is always hard to find original ones at a competitive price that will fit the space. Occasionally we may find a small set of suitable original chairs in the right style, but invariably there are never enough so we will have more copied to make up the required number.

ABOVE: A mahogany chest of drawers sits beneath a still life oil painting of fruit and flowers – a popular theme for dining room art. Chests of drawers are not typical dining room furniture, but can be useful for storing table linen or cutlery in specially lined drawers.

OPPOSITE: The table is set for a dinner for eight people using the clients' tableware, which was sourced with this room in mind. At night, with candlelight and the curtains closed, the room takes on a different hue, resembling a velvet-lined jewel box.

ABOVE: Detail of the silver cruets which form part of my client's collection of fine silver.

ABOVE RIGHT: Another group of fine silver items – a coffee pot, sugar bowls, jugs – which have been lovingly sourced and are regularly used.

OPPOSITE: A large Regency sideboard breaks up the long wall. Above it is one of a pair of still life paintings flanked by a pair of brass wall sconces in a similar style to the chandelier over the table.

I love to decorate formal dining rooms: it is one room where you can be bold and make a statement. Because these rooms are used more at night than during the day, strong vibrant colours come into their own. Shades of deep red exude warmth and glow in the candlelight. Oil paintings look great against red but during the day it can be a little overpowering, so using a softer coral colour could give you the best of both worlds. I also love greens and blues, but whatever you choose, it is always wise to look at a test in both daylight and artificial light to ensure your choice will work. White woodwork will also look very stark against strong colours, so consider painting doors, frames and skirtings (baseboards) in a darker colour, too.

family dining

LEFT: High ceilings allow for the use of a chair rail. Above this one is a green trellis wallpaper and below it a vivid green paint finish. The trellis on the ceiling was added to give more of a garden feel. The green paint emphasizes the design, with the central motif acting as a ceiling rose from which the chandelier hangs. Although the curtains do draw, roller shades in a complementary fabric are used, largely to block out the harsh sunlight at certain times of the day.

BELOW RIGHT: This view through to the kitchen shows the continuation of the travertine floor. French Provençal-style painted furniture adds to the informal country look.

For everyday dining you certainly do not want to get out the best china and glass and sit rather formally in the dining room, so an eating area in the kitchen, or better still in an adjoining breakfast room, is essential for modern-day living. Breakfast rooms are today's equivalent of eighteenth-century parlours, though without the servants! Many breakfast rooms are not just for dining but include a relaxed seating area complete with a television, an area to work and, most importantly with young children, an area to play and be supervised while a parent is cooking.

This breakfast room was designed for informal family dining. It is a bright, sunny room that leads off the main dining room but is reached though an open doorway from the kitchen. It is therefore conveniently close to the culinary action but slightly removed from cooking smells and noisy machines. The floor is travertine, which continues into the kitchen making the two rooms work as one. The table and chairs are placed in the curved window, so that the passageway from the dining room to the kitchen is kept clear.

daylight and candlelight

This stunning, formal, yet hugely inviting dining room is in a new-build house yet has all the qualities of an eighteenth-century room. With high ceilings and beautiful, full-height windows, the room is flooded with natural daylight and looks wonderful both by day and by night. The traditional Jacobean revival strapwork ceiling was inspired by the clients' previous home, as was the colour scheme. In fact, the fabrics, rug, table and chairs are all from there, and although this room is larger than the owners' previous dining room, the scale and proportions are perfect. The walls above the chair rail are panelled with plaster mouldings and painted in a warm, soft gold stipple finish with the mouldings wiped for emphasis. Below the chair rail, the walls are painted in oxblood red, which ties in with the curtains and at night adds a warm hue. Panelled mahogany doors add to the formality and are authentic to the period style.

ABOVE: One of a pair of custom-made carved gilt-wood console tables with Siena marble tops. They were made for the owners' previous home but work perfectly as a pair either side of the fireplace in this dining room. The gilding adds a nice contrast to the rest of the mahogany furniture.

LEFT: View of the stunning floor-to-ceiling windows with painted panelled reveals and rich oxblood red silk curtains.

OPPOSITE: The table is set for a formal dinner party with cream linen table mats and a beautiful custom-made dinner service. At night, the chandelier is not used – just candlelight from the candelabras and candlesticks. Picture lights over the oil paintings also add a soft glow. The mahogany dining table is an original Victorian piece, while the chairs were copied from an Irish design.

ABOVE: Detail showing a scagliola column and pilaster with ionic capitals which have been picked out in gold leaf. The elegant swagged pelmets are the perfect style and proportions for tall Georgian sash windows, and the custom-made fringe is enhanced with bobble hangers.

ABOVE: The exquisite ceiling painting was added to the room and is used in place of decorative plaster. There is no chandelier over the table as we did not want to ruin the painting, so candlelight and wall sconces provide light at night.

OPPOSITE: The large antique dining table can accommodate at least 16 people. Although in a different style, the high-back antique chairs add character to the room and have the back height that is necessary in such a tall room. The far end of the room with the large mahogany sideboard provides a perfect serving area.

a palladian gem

This traditional country house dining room is classic Palladian in style, evident in the cornice (cove), scagliola (imitation marble) columns, panelled shutters and oak plank floor, all of which were carefully restored. The ceiling painting, on canvas, was purchased by the owners and, once restored, was applied to the ceiling and framed with a custom-made wooden moulding gilded to look like an original frame. Surrounding the early nineteenth-century antique mahogany table, the chairs, which have painted and gilded legs, are upholstered in beautiful aged and embossed leather. The curtains are in a blue and gold brocade with trimmings custom-made to match. The walls are upholstered in a soft gold moiré and, below the chair rail, painted in a stippled finish to give depth and age.

a feast of chinoiserie

In a secluded area of London, the serene and elegant ground-floor dining room pictured here and overleaf is reminiscent of an eighteenth-century room inspired by the Far East. The contemporary silk wallpaper is still being hand-painted in China using centuries-old techniques and, although there are many standard designs to choose from, each commission is unique and fitted exactly to the room. The yellow silk curtain fabric was selected to look good in both daylight and artificial light, and the fringe and tassel tiebacks are in tones of green picked up from the walls. The gently curved swag and tails (cascades) hang gracefully from a gilded wooden pole.

Deliberately left white as a contrast to the walls, the carved wood fireplace is surmounted by a delicate oval gilt-wood mirror with Adam-style details, which is placed to reflect light from the chandelier. The table, made to fit the room, is a Regency-style reproduction with a twin-pedestal base and an apron edge. The two sets of antique chairs are in Chinese Chippendale style with drop-in seats which have been recovered.

LEFT: The colours of this room are suitable for both day and night use. Yellows and greens reflect natural light during the day, and the chinoiserie style gives an exotic feel by night.

ABOVE: Detail showing the delicate artwork and vibrant colours of the Chinese hand-painted silk wallpaper. The mirror is decorated with very fine gilded scrollwork in the style of the late 18th century.

RIGHT: Silver and porcelain are displayed on a Regency sideboard. Above it hangs an antique, hand-painted oriental panel in soft, faded colours. It is the perfect choice – any more dominant artwork would have competed with the hand-painted wallpaper.

BELOW: The tassel fringe and tiebacks are in several tones of green picked up from the walls, providing a good contrast to the yellow silk.

lush greenery

This well-proportioned dining room is in a home that was built about ten years ago in typical Palladian villa style, in a beautifully landscaped area of Atlanta. The main approach is from the hall through an impressive archway that conceals a pair of arched-top mahogany doors, known as pocket doors. The ceiling has applied plaster mouldings to break up the large expanse, and an English crystal chandelier hanging from the central rose. Owing to the ceiling height, a chair rail was installed which is also typical of the era. Above the chair rail hangs a specially commissioned green striped silk and below it is a marbleized paint finish with subtle green veins.

The end window provides a natural recess in which to place the antique sideboard while still allowing space for the curtains to be closed. These are in custom-made silk damask woven to match the walls, so that the overall effect is to blend with the vista, which is a mass of greenery.

LEFT: The silk damask curtain fabric has the same two tones of green as the wall covering.

OPPOSITE: A wide, full-length window overlooks the lush green garden. Sitting on an antique rug, the mahogany table, with an inlaid satinwood border, and the chairs, in Chippendale style, were all specially made for the room.

BELOW LEFT: The fireplace is a Georgian-style reproduction with green marble inlaid in the jambs and frieze. The mirror above reflects both daylight and candlelight.

BELOW: One of a pair of inlaid card tables, with oil paintings above, that sit symmetrically on either side of the arch.

red russian

Designed to impress and make a statement, this truly vibrant red dining room is inspired by a combination of classical references – Greek, Roman and Russian. The resulting eclectic look works particularly well in candlelight, when you have the impression of having stepped back into the eighteenth century. Because the ceiling is slightly domed, only the two long walls can have a cornice, which has a typical dentil design. On the end wall the focal point is a marble fireplace with a tall gilt mirror, which reflects the impressive arch opposite and the Russian chandelier. The table, which is French in style, is edged with ormolu. The painted chairs make the room a little less formal.

ABOVE: View from the dining room showing the grand arch with simulated stone keystones and marble pilasters, framing the sculptural spiral staircase in the hall beyond.

LEFT: The room has a wonderful view of parkland from the full-length windows, and the window treatments do not detract from it. A French commode sits between the windows, with a Georgian landscape by the Atlanta artist Peter Polites hanging above it.

OPPOSITE: The striking red-painted walls are great for showing off artwork and also supposedly for inducing an appetite – highly suitable for a dining room!

kitchens

Georgian kitchens were very much out of sight and out of mind –
a below-stairs warren of kitchens, sculleries, larders and pantries
where, in the grander houses, an army of cooks and servants
slaved over open fires and the owners rarely set foot. Today, of
course, the kitchen has become the hub of the home and the
preferred venue for casual family meals. The challenge in designing
kitchens today for Georgian-style homes is to produce something
timeless yet also ergonomically efficient, and bristling (unobtrusively)
with modern appliances.

LEFT: In spite of its vintage look, this new kitchen was carefully planned and each piece of
furniture custom-built to look informal and traditional. The range has a combination of
electric and gas burners, and a powerful extractor fan concealed by a wooden mantelpiece.
The tiles are an old-fashioned style: oblong in a cream crackle finish. A black gloss border
tile has been used to define them. Made from old wood, the large central table is used for
family meals and as a preparation area.

a kitchen for cooks

The owners of this kitchen are both enthusiastic cooks, so they were very involved in the design, layout and choice of furniture and equipment. I find that kitchen layouts are very personal. Everyone has their own habits and routines that need to be accommodated, and a designer must understand and respect this. Here, there is a huge amount of preparation space, with plenty of room for two cooks to work in their own space. Apart from the range and rotisserie, there is no exposed modern equipment, and the combination of pine, oak and painted wood creates an old-fashioned feel. The floor is a French limestone with a slate inset.

ABOVE: The painted wood fireplace was custom-made and lined in brick. The cupboard above is a fake facade installed as a feature. There are two Belfast sinks which rest on pine shelves, and the drainer and countertop are also in wood. No window treatments have been used, as the windows are beautiful just as they are and privacy is not an issue.

RIGHT: An antique pine dresser is the focal point of this wall, with its collection of old pots, teapots and plates that are all in regular use. The cupboards and glazed cabinets on either side were custom-made for glasses and tableware.

the utility room

ABOVE: The glazed upper section of the stable door can be positioned to direct passing Scottish breezes towards the laundry.

OPPOSITE: Deep Belfast sinks are good-looking, extremely practical and perfectly in keeping with this relaxed farmhouse style.

In an ideal world, every home would have a utility room, a laundry, a flower room and a mud room. This room, with its travertine floor, beech worktops and mimosa-coloured painted woodwork, looks as if it has served all these purposes for centuries, but it is in a new-build country house in Scotland. It leads off the kitchen shown on the previous spread. Natural sunlight streams in from all sides through large, unadorned windows that can be left open to welcome a breeze. Drying racks hanging from the ceiling allow laundry to be air-dried, a big plus for the environment and a kindness to clothes and household linens.

LEFT: View of one wall showing the purpose-built dresser unit that contains a huge amount of useful storage in a combination of glazed upper cupboards, plate racks, drawers and lower cupboards as well as a work surface.

RIGHT: This compact kitchen is a joy to use, as everything you need is easily to hand. The combination of the wood and painted finish of the cabinets creates a pleasing country style that is enhanced by the floral wallpaper and Austrian shades.

family kitchen

This country-style kitchen is, in fact, in a newly built home in a bustling US city. Very much a family kitchen, it is used regularly by both husband and wife, who enjoy cooking. The cabinets were selected from a standard range but the space was designed specifically for their use. As the house was a new-build, planning the kitchen was made easy – we were able to work out in advance what was required and allocate the space accordingly.

Although not large, it is a light and airy room that is very easy to work in, as everything is strategically placed for the working cook. The central island, which is painted in a contrasting blue, is the main preparation area with its own sink and an inset marble slab for pastry. The end forms a companionable breakfast bar with just enough room for two stools, a perfect spot for a cup of coffee.

bedrooms

A bedroom is a private place, but it was not always so. There was a time when it was quite the done thing to invite a chosen few to mingle around the bedside to witness one's morning routine. It was also a good opportunity to show off one's most expensive piece of furniture: the bed. Curtained beds were therefore very practical, allowing for moments of modesty as well as protection from draughts. In Georgian homes, the principal bedrooms in grand houses were large, comfortable and private, with separate dressing rooms. There would usually be an open fireplace, a desk and a place to sit and relax by a window. Just add central heating and it becomes the perfect recipe for a twenty-first-century retreat.

LEFT: Although the ceiling isn't high in the pretty London bedroom shown here and overleaf, the four-poster bed adds to the authentic feel. The chest at the end of the bed houses a very 21st-century remote-controlled television. Swing-arm wall lights within the bed provide good light for reading.

ABOVE: Also pictured on the previous spread, the four-poster mahogany bed was custom-made for the room. Its pelmet is trimmed with knotted rope and a matching bullion fringe.

ABOVE LEFT: The concealed jib door next to the bed has a closet behind it, cleverly ensuring that the line of the panelled wall is not interrupted. Antique floral prints with gilt frames sit within the panels.

LEFT: A three-tier mahogany whatnot with turned supports provides a good place to display beautiful, old, leather-bound books and antiques. It is a nice contrast against the painted original Georgian panelling, which has been picked out in shade of greens and creams.

OPPOSITE: Three windows look over the back garden. The central window has a pair of curtains with attached swags while the two side windows have single swagged curtains draped to the sides so as not to lose all the wall space between. The radiators below the windows are cased in so they do not interrupt the wall panelling. An area rug defines the comfortable seating area in front of the windows.

a room to dream in

Children's rooms should be special – a bit magical, without being too obviously babyish or driven by a theme that the child (never mind the parents) will quickly tire of. The decoration of this pretty top-floor bedroom was inspired by the eighteenth-century rococo style, when curves became all the rage, in reaction to all the straight lines of the Palladian era.

The daybed is built into an alcove that is panelled around the sides. Across the top, a carved, curved pelmet projects beyond the wardrobes to allow enough depth for a mattress. Within the cosy alcove, a pair of wall lights provides essential reading light for bedtime stories. The whole area is defined by the double-sided satin curtains, which create a magic and secret place for a child to sleep in.

ABOVE: The carved pelmet is decorated with a carved shell motif (a typical rococo motif), which is repeated above the wardrobes. An inset wood grille hides an air-conditioning vent.

OPPOSITE: The daybed, which is dressed with white linen, can also be used as a seating area in which to sit and read. Not only is it irresistible to children, but it is a good solution for rooms where space is at a premium. The painted panels of the alcove are picked out with a soft blue paint to tie in with the blue and white fabric of the bed skirt.

hand-painted silk

The green chinoiserie-style bedroom pictured here and overleaf is typical of the eighteenth-century fashion for hand-painted wall coverings in the 'Chinese taste'. In this room, the design was hand-painted onto silk panels that were specially measured and precisely planned for the room, taking into account the position of the windows, doors and fireplace so the continuity and scale of the design would not be compromised. The Italian-strung, or reefed, green silk curtains are topped with a gilded pelmet that provides a good contrast and makes a clean edge between the curtains, cornice (cove) and wallpaper. Blackout shades can be pulled down at night, so that the curtains do not have to be closed. Elegant bow-fronted window seats offer great places to watch the world go by, and on a practical level they conceal the radiators. Antique furniture pieces, all with softly curved lines, add weight to the otherwise very green room.

LEFT: A pretty and elegant chinoiserie-inspired bedroom provides a serene atmosphere and a welcome retreat in a bustling household. The combination of the antique furniture and the hand-painted silk wall covering gives the room an authentic 18th-century feel.

BELOW: A mantelshelf is the ideal place to display objects. Here, a pair of orchids adds splashes of colour and the crystal candelabras and antique scent bottles lend sparkle.

LEFT: The simple, elegant white marble mantelpiece provides a good focal point and a contrast to the busy walls. Over the mantelpiece is a gilt chinoiserie mirror that is perfectly suited to the room, both in scale and in style. With hand-painted wallpaper that is such a feature in its own right, there is no need to hang pictures. The gilt wall sconces were carefully chosen and positioned to appear as part of the wall painting rather than fight with it.

BELOW: A bow-fronted Georgian mahogany chest of drawers is placed in the alcove to the left of the fireplace, providing good storage for clothes and a useful surface for the display of personal collections and vases of fresh flowers.

floral calm

The bedroom shown here and overleaf is the main bedroom of a new-build Georgian-style home in Las Vegas. The house was built as a retreat from the get-up-and-go culture of that 24-hour city, and this bedroom is a deliberately calm and peaceful space. A fabric corona sits above the king-size bed, emphasizing the position of the bed on the long wall. The outer curtains are made of a pale floral chintz that is neither too busy nor too feminine, and the back curtain is in a silk check green to tie in with the walls. The headboard has a painted wood frame, but the padded and upholstered centre makes it more comfortable to lean against. Brass swing-arm wall lights provide good light for reading by.

ABOVE: You can just catch a glimpse of the en suite bathroom beyond the beautifully dressed bed with its matching bed linen.

LEFT: The flanking bedside tables are reproduction – finding genuine antique bedside commodes is often difficult.

Overlooking the garden and the golf course beyond, this upstairs bedroom is a lovely, peaceful, light room and is large enough to have a fireplace and reading area. The pale green of the walls is a cool and relaxing colour, ideal for a bedroom in a hot climate like that of Las Vegas. A printed floral chintz, used for the window and bed curtains and headboard, adds colour and brings the garden inside without totally dominating the room. The woodwork is painted in an off-white, making a good contrast to what could easily be a sea of green. The green walls are broken up not just by the white-painted woodwork, but also with paintings, mirrors and well-chosen pieces of furniture.

ABOVE: The two large French doors with panelled reveals lead out onto a balcony. They are dressed with chintz curtains and matching pelmets edged with a complementary fringe.

FAR LEFT: Over the fireplace on the side wall hangs a landscape oil painting. The upholstered stool at the end of the bed is a good way of filling the large space and provides welcome additional seating.

LEFT: Detail of the reproduction fireplace in white marble with matching hearth. Although the fire is not really required for heat as it would have been in the 18th century, it provides a pleasing focal point within any room.

A magnificent antique mahogany press on the wall opposite the fireplace adds height to the room as well as good additional storage space for clothes, which are mainly stored in an adjacent dressing room. The bed is most definitely the focal point of the room – it's hard for a bed as wide as this not to be. However, we decided to use a fabric corona to give the bed necessary height, rather than posts which would have intruded into the space.

Discreetly indirect, the lighting is a combination of chandelier, wall sconces and lamps. A bedroom rarely requires the provision of additional working light.

light-hearted lilac

Teenagers need bedrooms that are neither childish nor too grown-up. They need a space to express their own personalities and, while they often don't know what they want, they usually know what they don't want. This pale lilac bedroom was designed specifically for a teenage girl. It is fashionable but without being too girly or fussy, so she should be able to enjoy it for many years without tiring of the look.

The painted wrought iron bed is the main feature. It is placed between two of the four windows, which allow natural daylight to flood into the room. In order to keep the room light and not to encroach on the bed wall, the overlapping voile window treatments are translucent and airy – behind them are roller shades so the room can be darkened at night.

Painted furniture gives the room a young, light-hearted feel. Fortunately, there is a separate dressing room so it is not necessary to have lots of built-in storage space in the bedroom itself.

ABOVE: A painted armoire with a French provincial look about it conceals a television – a very necessary element for a teenager's space, but one that would have spoiled the look of this pretty and serene bedroom.

LEFT: This bedroom is in a home in Las Vegas, and the two-tone colour scheme of lilac and off-white is ideal for the hot and sunny climate.

youthful exuberance

This flamboyant bedroom was designed for a teenage girl with a very definite idea of her own style. It is situated in a beautiful country house in Georgia that has been comprehensively renovated but retains many original features. The walls above the room's chair rail are upholstered in a specially dyed lilac silk, and below the rail there is a paint finish in a lighter shade. The main fabric used in the bedroom is an embroidered silk, while a deeper purple silk/cotton mix has been used for the secondary curtains.

The room has three windows facing north and west, and so the only position in which the bed could be sited was between the two north-facing windows, opposite the fireplace. Because of the high ceilings, a four-poster was the natural choice, and it was custom-made for the room with carved mahogany end posts. The remainder of the frame was left as natural wood because it was to be covered in fabric and the finish would not be on display.

RIGHT: The bed is dressed in silk fabrics edged with a fine glass-bead trim that is also used on the window curtains. The upholstered headboard has a ruched border in the contrast silk. Scatter pillows and a wool throw complete the pretty picture.

OPPOSITE: This is a very sophisticated room, but the fabrics and colour add a younger touch and the whole is made less formal by the brightly coloured wool rugs beside the bed. The window treatments are hung to one side to allow more space for the bed.

colonial style

This colonial-style bedroom was created in an annex of a newly built house. It has a really interesting cathedral ceiling, open to the eaves and with wonderful oak beams laced through it. A combination of different woods gives the impression that this room has evolved slowly through time. The beams are structural, but they also define the bed area. They have been left in their natural state so that they can age naturally.

The mahogany screen behind the bed, which looks like something you would find in an early nineteenth-century chapel, acts as a half-wall. The bed is positioned against it, facing the window, and on the other side is a convenient run of built-in shelves and closets. All the furniture and accessories are colonial in style, and we used shutters rather than curtains at the sash windows to complete the overall look. A Japanese hot tub and a rustic shower are part of the en suite bathroom arrangements – a bit unexpected, but working well in this eclectic rural retreat.

ABOVE LEFT: A stone corner fireplace forms a focal point and above it is a flat-screen television concealed behind folding doors.

TOP: A Japanese-style wooden bath is filled from wall-mounted taps (faucets) set into a slate surround. A special step enables the user to get in and out with a degree of grace!

ABOVE: A separate shower tiled in rustic stone and mosaic tiles sits in the area behind the mahogany screen.

RIGHT: Wall-mounted reading lights are installed on the screen. The lighting in general is kept low and indirect, with table lamps providing atmospheric pools of light.

golden glow

This warm and welcoming golden bedroom with its glowing wooden floor and gilded touches could have come straight from an authentic Georgian house, but it is, in fact, a guest bedroom in a newly built country house. The four-poster bed, which was specially commissioned for the room, is dressed with drapes to match the window curtains in a contemporary cream embroidered silk, similar to a traditional crewelwork fabric. There is a lovely symmetry about this room and a pleasing colour palette – from the rhythm of the windows to the glow of the inlaid armoire and the lovely oil painting over the marble fireplace.

ABOVE: A large contemporary rug defines the space and breaks up the large expanse of wooden floorboards. The walls above the wainscot are upholstered in fabric.

OPPOSITE: The four-poster bed, a staple of the 18th-century bedroom, is a focal point in this lovely guest bedroom. The fireplace, complete with a modern gas fire, provides a cosy atmosphere on cold, rainy winter nights.

classic toile de jouy

A very popular fabric design in the eighteenth century, toile de Jouy (literally, cloth from Jouy en Josas, a small French town close to Versailles) has been produced there since the late 1700s. It works well in profusion because it is basically a repeated design, usually a pastoral scene, in a single colour on a cream or white background. Here, a powder blue and cream toile was teamed with a plain matching blue fabric and contrasted with white upholstery and bed linen. The combination of blue and white is fresh and works well as it is neither overtly feminine nor masculine, and it goes very well with natural wood. It is a classic and relaxed look, perfect for a guest bedroom.

ABOVE: The American four-poster bed has a mahogany headboard rather than an upholstered one. Brass swing-arm wall lights are strategically placed through the back curtain to provide good reading light in bed. The sofa at the foot anchors the bed position and fills what would otherwise be a large space.

ABOVE LEFT: An 18th-century-style bedroom with a classic blue and cream toile de Jouy fabric used throughout, including in the en suite bathroom.

RIGHT: Placed between the two windows, this mahogany writing table with a mirror above it makes a good dressing table.

pretty and pastoral

This pretty green corner guest bedroom in a new-build house in Atlanta is decorated with a chinoiserie-style toile de Jouy fabric that gives the room a country feel while remaining sophisticated. The windows have two sets of curtains – the secondary curtains, in a green silk, are drawn at night, leaving the patterned drapes to frame the window. A bright touch comes from the oil painting on the far wall. Guest bedrooms should reflect the general ambience of the house while not overwhelming visitors with personal detail. This bedroom is a perfect example of thoughtful and welcoming comfort.

ABOVE: The walls of the guest bedroom are covered in green silk, a treatment that was still very fashionable in the 18th century, even though wallpapers had become increasingly available.

supremely stylish

ABOVE: This bedroom has tall ceilings so it can easily accommodate a four-poster bed. The bed's elegant turned columns are in a dark-stained wood that is echoed in the arched double doors.

This is the main bedroom of the newly designed and built Atlanta house. The bedroom is, unusually, situated on the ground floor, with three full-length windows on the wall opposite the bed to take advantage of the wonderful views overlooking the private garden.

A yellow Fortuny-style material, a type of fabric that originated in Venice, has been used in the room, creating a bright, cheerful look well suited to the elegant furnishings. Comfortable seating is a real luxury in a master bedroom. It turns the bedroom into a private space for self-indulgent relaxation.

bathrooms

In the absence of plumbing, Georgians took their baths in tin tubs set in front of bedroom fireplaces while jugs of hot water and chamber pots were discreetly ferried up and down the back stairs by servants. Obviously, few of us would wish to recreate this level of authenticity, but in a house decorated in Georgian style, an ultra-modern decor, even in the bathroom, would be inappropriate, so a compromise is needed. Equally, to establish a bathroom in a period house that was never designed to house one is a challenge. In many original Georgian homes, spare bedrooms are subdivided to provide small bathrooms, but that does ruin the proportions. I would prefer to sacrifice a whole bedroom and create within it a generous, luxurious space in traditional style.

LEFT: The bathroom shown here and overleaf is large enough to place a free-standing bath in the middle of the room. However, it was essential to establish the exact location before installing the pipework, as the bath taps (faucets) are exposed and floor-mounted. The wood plank floor was newly installed and sealed to protect it from any water. A flat-screen television was sunk within the panelled wall and bordered with wood trim to tie it in with the rest of the room. Each window has two single decorative curtains, which are pulled back to opposite sides, with voile under-curtains providing some privacy. The mahogany chest of drawers adds a classic feel, as well as providing useful storage space.

ABOVE: Nickel wall lights with hurricane shades in etched glass are used throughout the room to provide atmospheric light. Downlights in the ceiling give a good level of general light.

ABOVE RIGHT: A useful storage cupboard with shelves above is built into the alcove to the left of one of the sinks. The paintwork has been dragged in tones of green and cream.

RIGHT: An antique gilded sofa opposite the bath is a good perching point to sit and chat while your partner lounges in the bath in front of the fire. It has also become a favoured cosy spot for the resident Persian cat.

OPPOSITE: As well as a bath, there is a large shower with frameless glass walls. The top of the shower tray is level with the wood floor, minimizing the visual impact of the shower. The large 'rain' showerhead delivers a deluge of water while the secondary, wall-mounted head is good for washing down the walls and glass.

delicate chinoiserie

Leading off the pretty chinoiserie green bedroom featured on pages 124–7, the London town house bathroom pictured here and overleaf feels like a room in the country. The theme runs through the entire house, so it seemed only fitting to continue it here. Chinoiserie was an asymmetric decorative style that reached its peak of popularity in the mid-eighteenth century. Based on an idealized and imaginary vision of China, it was inspired by images on imported Chinese porcelain, hand-painted wallpapers, lacquerwork and landscape painting.

This bathroom has a strong focal point – the bath itself. Double-ended and encased in a curved panelled frame with a marble surround and splashback, it

sits opposite a built-in vanity unit. A painted overmantel mirror with gilded gesso carvings reflects light from the window. This is a very practical and decorative solution to what to do with the wall space above a bath – framed pictures might be ruined by water splashes.

The window treatment follows those of the adjoining bedroom, with voile under-curtains for privacy. A pretty upholstered window seat conceals a radiator and provides a spot where a parent can perch while youngsters are having a bath. Antique hand-painted bird pictures are hung on one side of the window, and on the other side there is a corner shower stall.

LEFT: Double-ended baths are good for sharing, as no one has to sit at the tap end. This bath is strategically placed so that the occupant can lie and soak while contemplating the veiled view from the window.

RIGHT: An antique gilt chair, which is upholstered in beige linen, is placed near the bath, becoming a useful parking place for towels or for dressing gowns.

LEFT: An elaborate crystal and gilt mirror-stand holds antique potion bottles. It's a lovely piece that adds a dash of sparkle and wit.

OPPOSITE: A custom-built vanity unit houses two inset sinks while providing useful storage. The taps (faucets) are set into the marble top, which has a small upstand to protect the walls. Wall lights give additional lighting for applying make-up and for shaving.

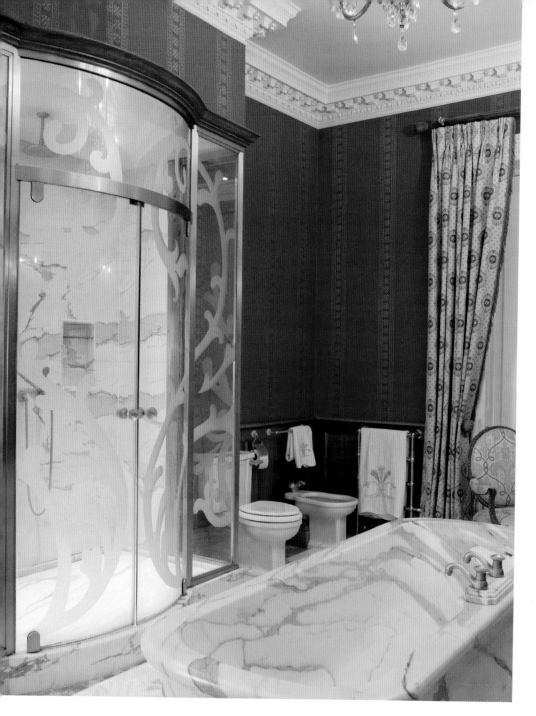

classic exuberance

This large country bathroom has wonderful proportions and a high ceiling, so it was easy to treat it flamboyantly. The starting point was the carved marble bath, which had to be winched in by crane via the window in a specially made cradle. The large steam shower was also a big challenge as it had to be a totally sealed unit and the mechanism for the steam had to be accessible for servicing. We achieved this by placing the complex plumbing above the shower, with access from the dressing room behind. The large glass doors were custom-engraved with whimsical trailing foliage loosely representing seaweed or coral. The rest of the room is more classical, with wainscot panelling in walnut, and the walls above are hand-painted and stencilled.

ABOVE LEFT AND TOP: Two structural challenges: a steam shower and a carved marble bath with gold taps (faucets).

ABOVE: Cut-glass door handles provide a subtle contrast to the walnut woodwork.

OPPOSITE: One of a pair of custom-made vanity units in walnut with marble tops, which sit either side of the original Georgian fireplace. The beautiful free-standing mirrors above the sinks were made by a local craftsman. Antique ormolu and crystal wall lights add sparkle.

planning and panelling

Installing new bathrooms into upstairs former bedrooms is a challenge in more ways than one. One extremely important consideration is the strength of the floor. A bathroom floor has to be strong enough to take the weight of heavy items such as baths and showers and maybe stone or tile wall and floor coverings, as well as the not inconsiderable weight of the bathwater. In many cases the floor will need to be strengthened with steel beams, and floor levels may need to be altered to accommodate drainage and all the associated plumbing. Bathrooms require a great deal of advance planning.

This internal bathroom was a case in point. It is part of a room that was subdivided to create two new en suite bathrooms. New proportions had to be devised and two sets of complex plumbing had to be discreetly hidden behind the new walls.

LEFT: The cistern (tank) of the toilet is concealed behind a panel as is the pipework for the bidet, leaving clean lines. The taps (faucets) and accessories are in a brushed nickel finish.

RIGHT: This en suite bathroom has a masculine and traditional feel thanks to the natural wood panels and ebony mouldings. A brown marble splashback, edged with a wooden moulding, continues around the bath and sink.

pretty in pink

This exotic pink bathroom was designed for a teenage girl and has everything she might need: a bath and separate shower as well as toilet, bidet and vanity unit. The starting point was colour – in this case the delicate pale pink and grey-veined marble used for the bath surround, vanity top and shower. In order to show off the marble and enhance the subtle colour, we used borders of mother-of-pearl mosaic tile which really help bring it all to life. The walls are in a polished plaster finish. Apart from being an excellent practical surface for moist areas, it has a lovely soft glow – just perfect for this young, fresh and pretty room.

ABOVE LEFT: The stone tile floor has an inset mother-of-pearl border that reflects the shape of the dome above.

LEFT: The vanity unit is built into a recess. It has a curved centre and curved doors with inset borders of mother-of-pearl. There are narrow shelves on either side for towel storage, and the marble top defines the whole unit.

OPPOSITE: Two mirrors, both bordered with mother-of-pearl, help reflect the natural light, as the room has only one small window. Wall lights are mounted directly onto the mirror, which also helps to reflect light.

LEFT: A wide pedestal sink with brushed-chrome stand complete with towel rails gives this bathroom a contemporary feel. The mirror above it is a shallow cabinet inset into the wall, and the wall lights give additional light for shaving.

OPPOSITE: The free-standing bath has an enamel interior but the exterior is finished to look like tin. The taps (faucets) are wall-mounted, and the marble corner shelf provides a convenient spot for a soap dish.

contemporary chrome

In order to give a bathroom a contemporary cutting edge without pulling too far in directions unsuitable for the traditional Georgian home, it is possible to find or to commission bathroom fixtures that are totally classic and clean-cut. Free-standing pieces are often a good choice, as they tend to be more sculptural than built-ins. Add to these a touch of chrome, plus natural surfaces such as polished plaster, marble, stone or plain tile, and you have a bathroom that feels modern and classic at the same time. The best of both worlds, in fact. This en suite bathroom has a successful contemporary and masculine feel that is perfect for its occupant,

a teenage boy. A square shower stall with two glass sides is built to the left of the window – essential for any boy in a morning rush to get to school. The shapely freestanding bath is strategically placed in front of the window, which makes a great spot for more leisurely bathing.

The marble floor tiles have been laid diagonally to make the room appear larger, and smartly edged with a darker, contrasting marble. The walls are also clad in marble up to chair-rail height and finished with a moulded marble border. The walls are in polished plaster, a practical and contemporary finish.

LEFT: The built-in toilet is a so-called 'thunder box', which is encased in oak panelling. The cistern (tank) is concealed in the wall behind, and shelves set into the wall above provide a useful display area for books and decorative objects.

OPPOSITE: This sink is built into a vanity unit with a slate worktop and upstand. The decorative taps (faucets) and spout are finished in bronze. The 'cushion' mirror over it is an antique and the uplights flanking it throw light onto the wall above them.

grandfather's thunderbox

This old-fashioned 'gents' cloakroom' is reminiscent of one I remember as a child in my grandparents' home. Created just a few years ago in an English country house that is partly Palladian, this is a masculine space that provides practical, up-to-date facilities. An anteroom houses the sink, and both spaces are panelled in oak up to chair-rail height. Above the panelling, the walls are papered in an architectural toile de Jouy-style paper in a sympathetic colourway. The floor is new limestone – a warm and inviting flooring material that flows through from an original flagstone hallway.

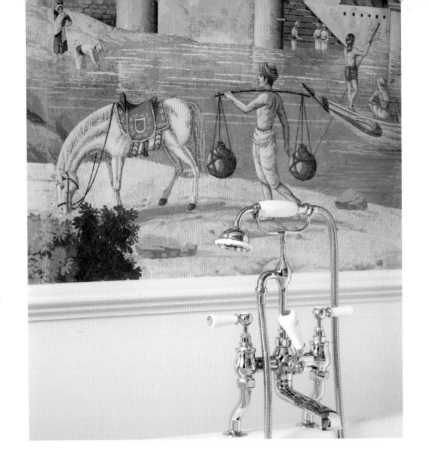

OPPOSITE: This country-style bathroom is large enough to accommodate both a free-standing bath and a modern shower. In my view this is more practical, providing you have the space, than installing a shower within the bath and having to cope with a glass screen or shower curtain. The shower tiles are ceramic but are in a finish to simulate limestone. On the walls, an exotic, hand-painted wallpaper depicts an old-fashioned Indian colonial scene. The muted tones make it look as if it has faded gracefully over the years.

RIGHT: Detail of the polished nickel bath taps (faucets), which are mounted on the rim of the bath rather than being buried in the wall, so they do not intrude into the mural.

BELOW: Custom-made for the room, the vanity unit and mirror provide practical storage space without looking too utilitarian.

masculine tradition

ABOVE RIGHT: The traditional-style toilet is partially concealed in a recessed alcove – with a magnificent scenic view of the garden!

OPPOSITE: The practical yet elegant vanity unit was custom-made in mahogany and has a marble top into which the basin is set. Crystal drawer-pulls make a nice contrast to all the dark wood. Mahogany shutters complete the scene and provide privacy as well as filtering out the harsh Atlanta sun.

In a new-build Georgian-style home, planning and plumbing are a great deal easier. All the panelling and joinery for this masculine-style bathroom was custom-designed and made for the room, based on traditional eighteenth-century designs. There is no bath in this area, but a clever double-door shared shower unit leads from here – the husband's area – through to the wife's domain, where she has a bath and her own vanity unit. The vanity in this bathroom is built extra-high to accommodate the tall owner, and a stepped-back 'break-front' shape ensures it fits in neatly beside the window. The top and upstand are marble, while the taps (faucets) and accessories are in silver nickel. Although there are practical downlights in the bathroom, the wall sconces and antique chandelier add an authentic eighteenth-century feel.

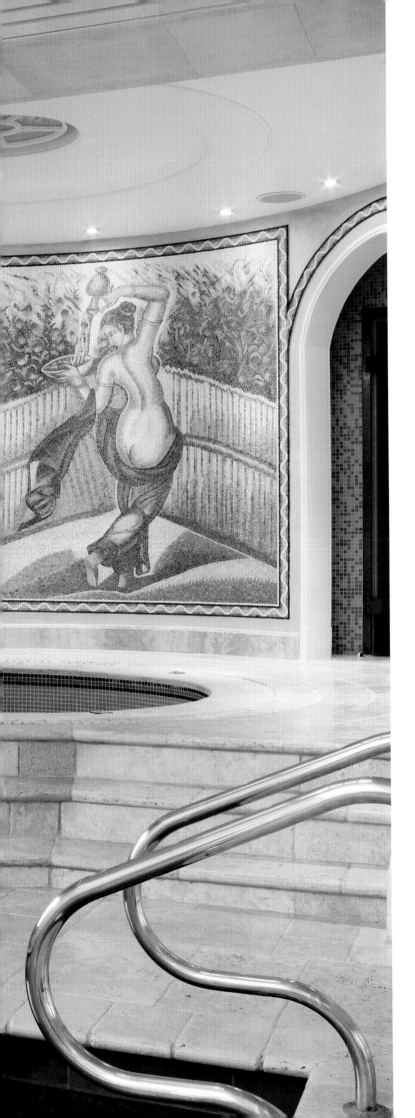

outside in

In this chapter are gathered together the type of hedonistic rooms – a spa and an indoor pool – undreamed of in Georgian times. Also included are exteriors of some newly built Georgian-style homes, which I hope will prove that modern architects are every bit as adept as their Georgian counterparts in placing a house in a landscape.

LEFT: Built as an extension to an existing house, this indoor swimming pool links two wings together and completes the fourth side of an interior quadrangle which is, in fact, the older part of a primarily late Georgian house. The raised end is dedicated to a spa area incorporating a jacuzzi, steam room, plunge pool and shower. The curved walls act as a screen and create a focal point from the pool. Inspired by an old painting, the commissioned mosaic has been carefully created in small tesserae to give depth. The border follows the lines of the walls and arches, and two other panels are left blank for future artwork.

LEFT: The ceiling has a large roof light with a secondary glazed flat surface comprising glass-engraved panels that make the space more practical for both heat conservation and cleaning. The pool is lined with green slate tiles that are softer than a bright blue mosaic would be and more in keeping with the outside. The main floor is travertine and the walls are in a Venetian plaster that is applied onto a wire mesh with the colour already included. The wall lights were specially commissioned and in this damp environment need to be watertight for safety reasons. The wooden doors open onto a pretty Japanese-style garden.

ABOVE: The cloister passage leads off the pool area and looks onto a pretty internal courtyard. Underfloor heating (radiant heat) is used throughout, which explains the grilles in front of the doors. A talented craftsman made the wall lights and the design is replicated in the chandelier over the seating area.

RIGHT: This seating area, which leads off the pool, is in a part of the house dating back to medieval times. As it would have been very difficult to glaze the arches individually, a large glass screen has been erected on the inside wall, allowing the full extent of the original arches to be seen. The combination of exposed stone walls and a stone floor adds to the outdoor feel, as does the natural wicker furniture.

ABOVE: View of the back of a Georgian-style house built in the United States with a traditional stucco finish and with stone quoins and architraves. The main rooms are at first-floor level, creating a *piano nobile*, and the design is similar to a Palladian villa. The slate roof is hipped, and a large bowed section breaks up the line.

RIGHT: View of the front facade with its pedimented central section and portico. A curved double staircase in stone leads up to the *piano nobile*, and the first and second floors are divided by a stone string course.

ABOVE: Stone steps and balustrades flank this pretty tiered cascade, inspired by English gardens. It links the main house to the pool area and the orangery above. The water travels under the flat grass lawn in a channel and emerges into the bottom level, from where it is pumped back up to the top.

RIGHT: The impressive back facade of a new house built in the United States out of limestone, with all the features of an early English Georgian manor. The house sits nestled in beautiful landscaped gardens and looks as if it has been there for centuries.

index

acknowledgments

The author would like to thank all her clients and friends both named and unnamed who have very kindly agreed for their houses to be featured in this book. Their co-operation was greatly appreciated.

The author would also like to thank the photographer Chris Drake for his professionalism and sense of humour – he was a pleasure to work with – and Rose Hammick for her styling.

My thanks also go to my editor Alex Parsons – who should by now be well versed in unravelling my sometimes disjointed text! – as well as, of course, to all the team at CICO books.

Many thanks to the following people for allowing us to photograph their homes:

Sally Cooney and Tom Henson: their home and guest house in Atlanta, GA; interior design by Patricia McLean. (Patricia McLean Interiors, Inc., 3179 Maple Drive Suite 10, Atlanta, GA 30305, Tel: 404 266 9772, Fax: 404 266 9773, mcleanints@mindspring.com, www.mcleaninteriors.com)

Julie and Jim Richard: their home in Atlanta, GA.

Rodney and Emily Cook: Alexandra Park, their home and park in Atlanta, GA; interior design by Rodney Mims Cook, with thanks also to Henrietta. (Rodney Mims Cook, Tel: 404 237 8970, Fax: 404 237 1707, rcook@thenmf.org, www.rodneymimscook.com)